YOU CAN DO IT

Published 2024

FiNGERPRINT!

An imprint of **Prakash Books India Pvt. Ltd**

113/A, Darya Ganj,
New Delhi-110 002
Email: info@prakashbooks.com/sales@prakashbooks.com

Fingerprint Publishing

@FingerprintP

@fingerprintpublishingbooks

www.fingerprintpublishing.com

ISBN: 978 93 5856 225 5

To.....................

From....................

To do or not to do, that is the question.

We are all waiting—waiting for inspiration, for the right moment, or for someone to believe in us.

But in this waiting game, there are no winners. Either you can wait around for people to have faith in you or you can have faith in yourself and take that leap!

Talent, opportunities, and luck are important, but what separates extraordinary people from the ordinary is taking that first step of believing in themselves.

The challenges you face along the way can be daunting, but with hard work, perseverance, and determination . . . You Can Do It!

"The question isn't who
is going to let me; it's who
is going to stop me."

AYN RAND

"MAN NEEDS HIS DIFFICULTIES BECAUSE THEY ARE NECESSARY TO ENJOY SUCCESS."

A. P. J. Abdul Kalam

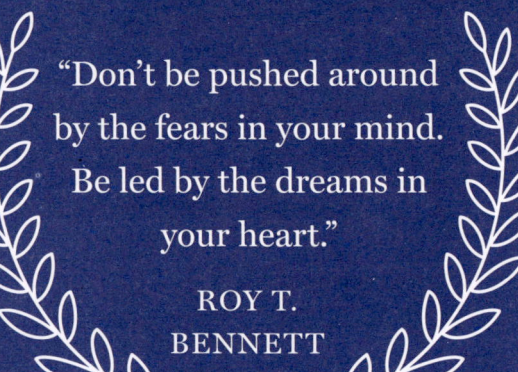

"Don't be pushed around
by the fears in your mind.
Be led by the dreams in
your heart."

ROY T.
BENNETT

"Pearls don't lie on the seashore. If you want one, you must dive for it."

CHINESE PROVERB

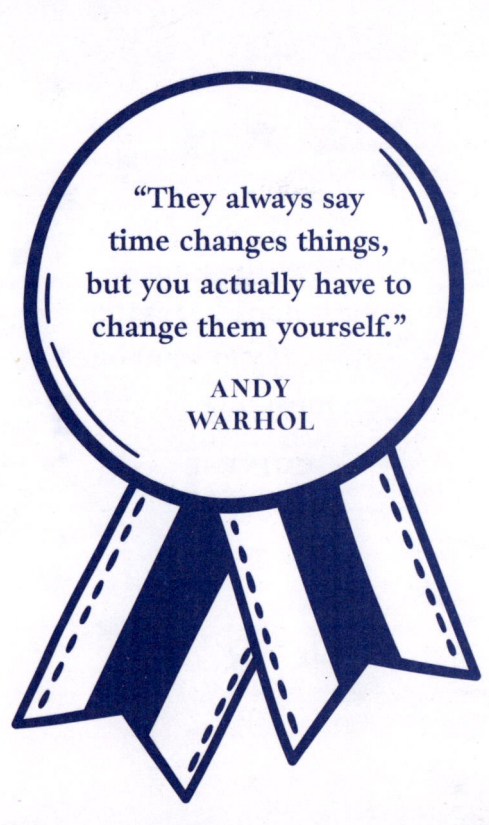

"They always say
time changes things,
but you actually have to
change them yourself."

ANDY
WARHOL

"THE BEST WAY TO
PREDICT THE FUTURE
IS TO CREATE IT."

Peter F. Drucker

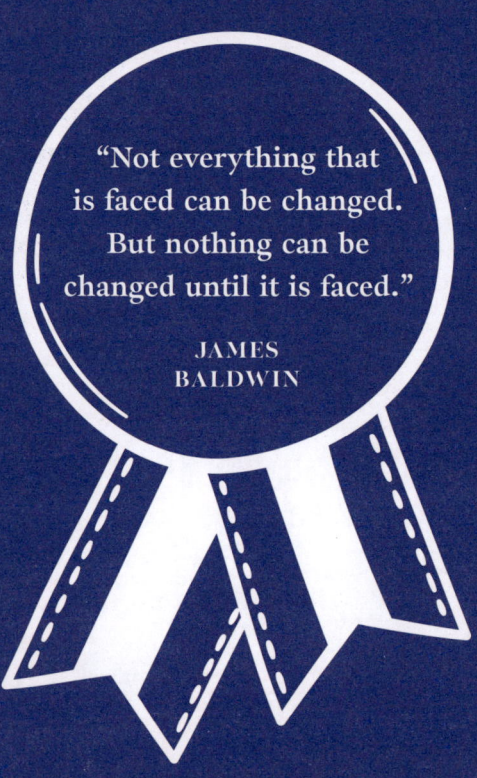

"Not everything that is faced can be changed. But nothing can be changed until it is faced."

JAMES
BALDWIN

"I am only an average
man, but, by George,
I work harder at it
than the average man."

THEODORE ROOSEVELT

"If you are too careful,
you are so occupied
in being careful that
you are sure to stumble
over something."

GERTRUDE STEIN

"Amateurs wait for inspiration.
The rest of us just get
up and go to work."

CHUCK CLOSE

"Don't go around saying
the world owes you a living.
The world owes you nothing.
It was here first."

MARK TWAIN

"ANYONE CAN DO ANY AMOUNT
OF WORK, PROVIDED IT ISN'T
THE WORK HE IS SUPPOSED TO
BE DOING AT THAT MOMENT."
ROBERT BENCHLEY

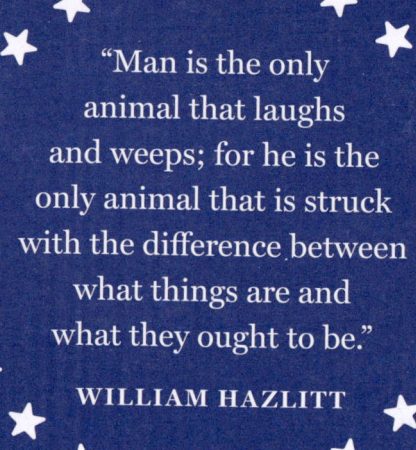

"Man is the only
animal that laughs
and weeps; for he is the
only animal that is struck
with the difference between
what things are and
what they ought to be."

WILLIAM HAZLITT

"THERE ARE NO HOPELESS
SITUATIONS; THERE ARE ONLY
PEOPLE WHO HAVE GROWN
HOPELESS ABOUT THEM."
CLARE BOOTHE LUCE

"A dream does not
become reality through
magic; it takes sweat,
determination and
hard work."

COLIN POWELL

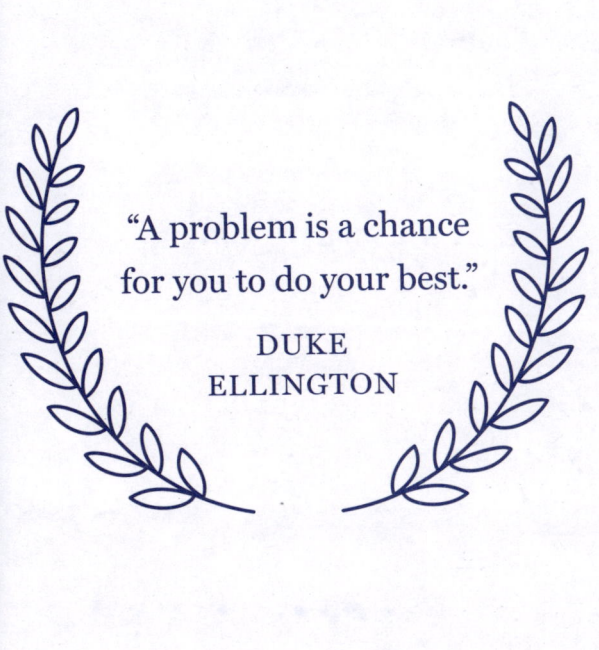

"A problem is a chance
for you to do your best."

DUKE
ELLINGTON

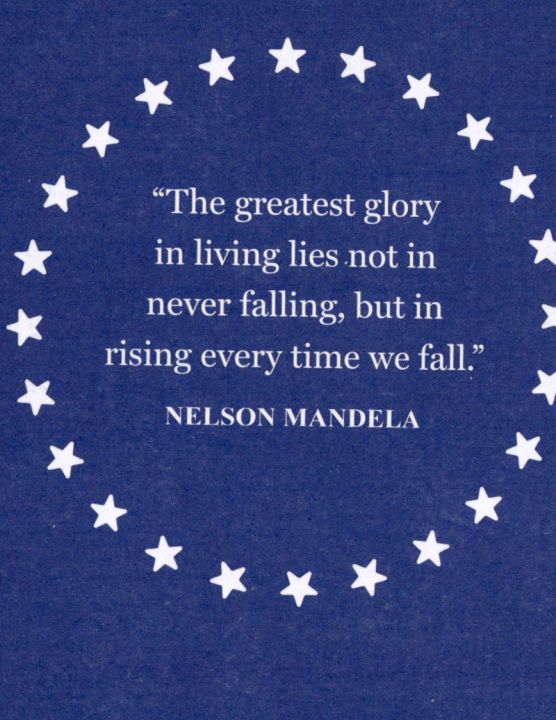

"The greatest glory
in living lies not in
never falling, but in
rising every time we fall."

NELSON MANDELA

"PAY NO ATTENTION
TO WHAT THE CRITICS SAY.
A STATUE HAS NEVER BEEN
ERECTED IN HONOR
OF A CRITIC."
Jean Sibelius

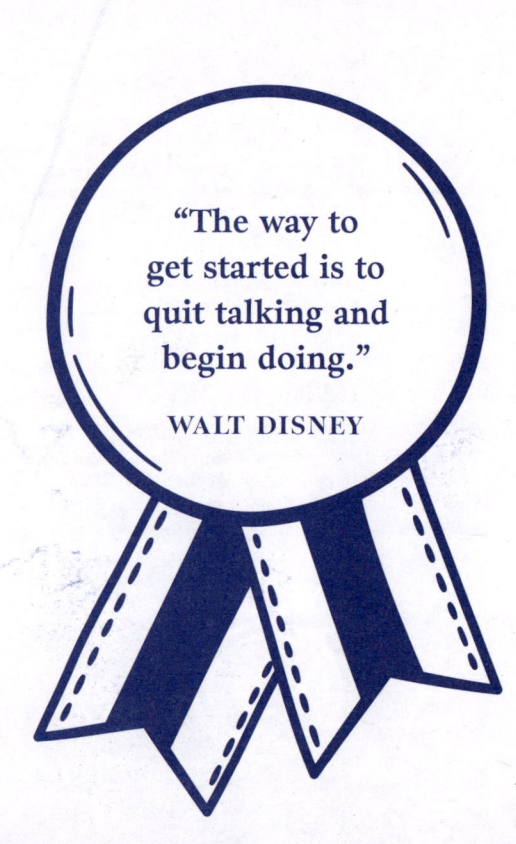

"The way to
get started is to
quit talking and
begin doing."

WALT DISNEY

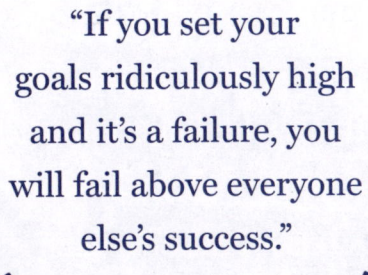

"If you set your
goals ridiculously high
and it's a failure, you
will fail above everyone
else's success."

**JAMES
CAMERON**

"The future belongs to those who believe in the beauty of their dreams."

ELEANOR ROOSEVELT

"Do not go where the path may lead, go instead where there is no path and leave a trail."

RALPH WALDO EMERSON

"LIFE IS NEVER FAIR,
AND PERHAPS IT
IS A GOOD THING
FOR MOST OF US
THAT IT IS NOT."

OSCAR WILDE

"If you want to achieve
greatness, stop asking
for permission."

ANONYMOUS

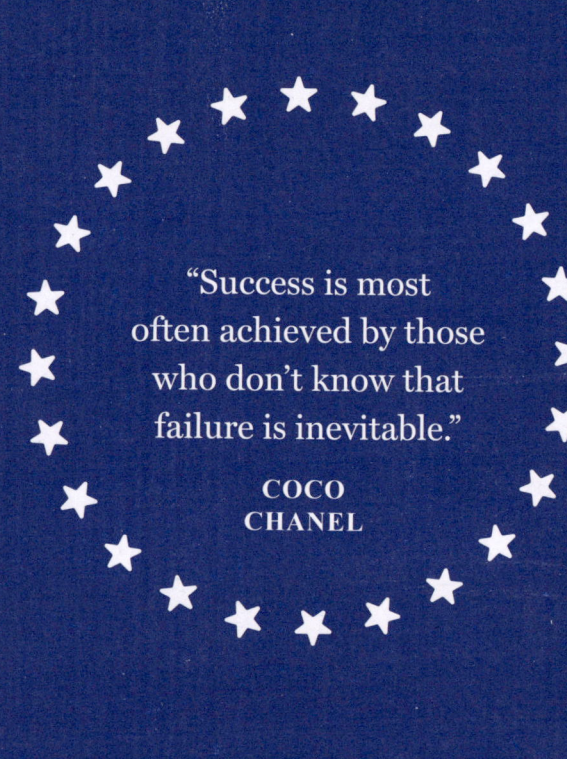

"Success is most
often achieved by those
who don't know that
failure is inevitable."

COCO
CHANEL

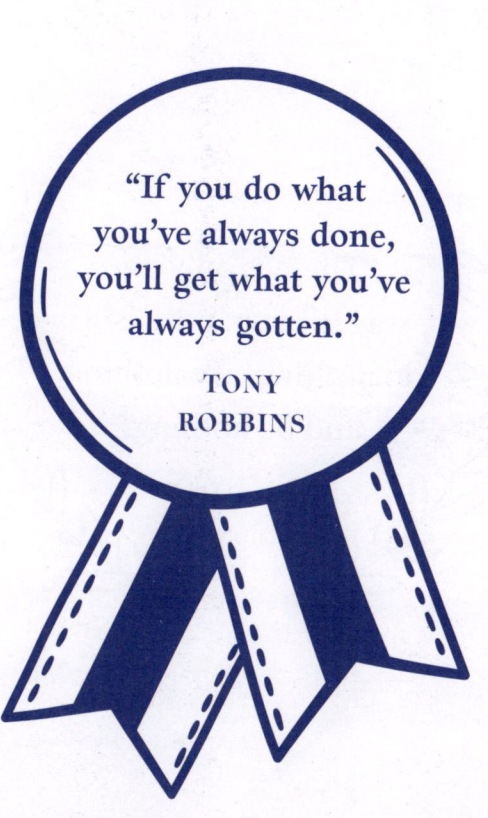

"If you do what you've always done, you'll get what you've always gotten."

TONY ROBBINS

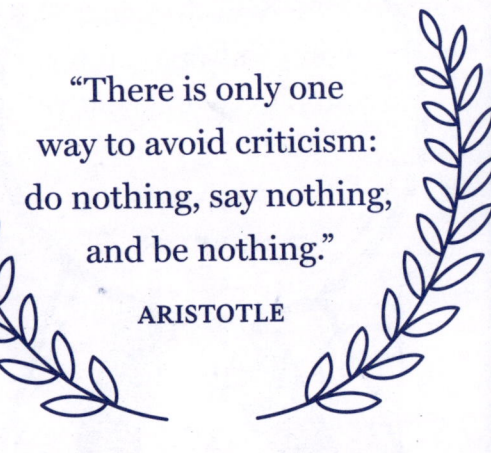

"There is only one
way to avoid criticism:
do nothing, say nothing,
and be nothing."

ARISTOTLE

"WHEN I LET GO OF WHAT I AM,
I BECOME WHAT I MIGHT BE."

Lao Tzu

"If you're offered a seat on a rocket ship, don't ask what seat! Just get on."

SHERYL SANDBERG

"Only those who will risk
going too far can possibly
find out how far one can go."

T. S. ELIOT

"Only those who play to win.
Only those who risk to win.
History favors risk-takers.
Forgets the timid.
Everything else is commentary."

IVETA CHERNEVA

"I always did something I was a little not ready to do. I think that's how you grow. When there's that moment of 'Wow, I'm not really sure I can do this' and you push through those moments, that's when you have a breakthrough."

MARISSA MAYER

"IF YOU DON'T BUILD YOUR
DREAM, SOMEONE ELSE
WILL HIRE YOU TO HELP
THEM BUILD THEIRS."

DHIRUBHAI AMBANI

"A failure is not always a mistake. It may simply be the best one can do under the circumstances. The real mistake is to stop trying."

B.F. SKINNER

"AND THE DAY CAME WHEN THE RISK TO REMAIN TIGHT IN A BUD WAS MORE PAINFUL THAN THE RISK IT TOOK TO BLOSSOM."

Anaïs Nin

HOW TO WORK HARD
WHEN YOU ARE NOT FEELING IT!

* Don't work hard, work smart. Putting in long and strenuous hours is not the way to go about work. Instead, focus on being effective and efficient.

* Take breaks. Resting and rejuvenating is as important as working hard.

* Celebrate small wins. Rewarding yourself is the key to motivation.

* Remember your 'why'. We all have a purpose and when times get tough, that purpose serves as a guiding light.

* Any work is not a marathon but a sprint. Remember, Rome was not built in a day.

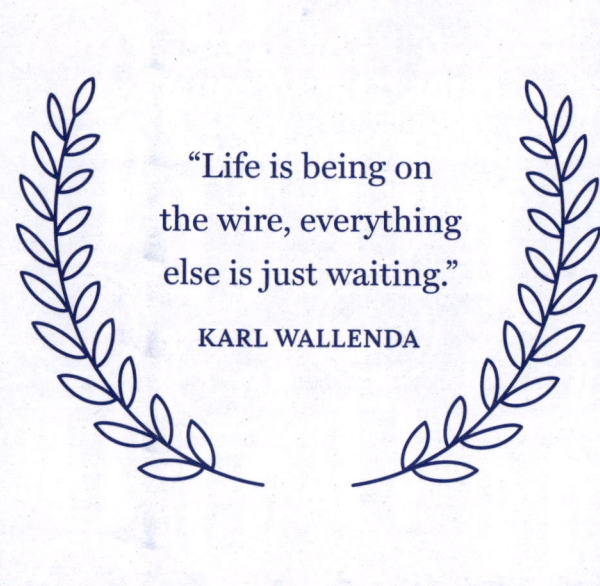

"Life is being on
the wire, everything
else is just waiting."

KARL WALLENDA

"THE FIRST STEP TOWARD
SUCCESS IS TAKEN WHEN YOU
REFUSE TO BE A CAPTIVE OF
THE ENVIRONMENT IN WHICH
YOU FIRST FIND YOURSELF."

Mark Caine

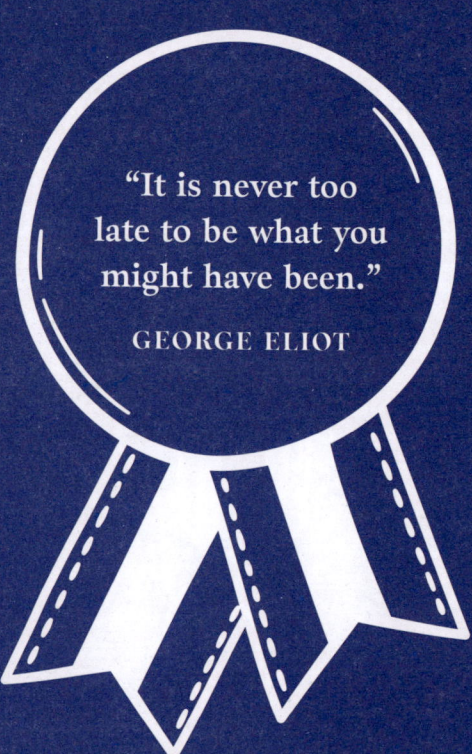

"It is never too late to be what you might have been."

GEORGE ELIOT

"Nobody gets to live life backward.
Look ahead—that's where
your future lies."

ANN LANDERS

"You can't outwit fate by standing on the sidelines placing little side bets about the outcome of life. Either you wade in and risk everything you have to play the game or you don't play at all. And if you don't play you can't win."

JUDITH MCNAUGHT

"Often the difference
between a successful person
and a failure is not one has
better abilities or ideas, but
the courage that one has
to bet on one's ideas, to take
a calculated risk and to act."

ANDRÉ MALRAUX

"You can't connect the dots looking forward; you can only connect them looking backwards. So you have to trust that the dots will somehow connect in your future. You have to trust in something; your gut, destiny, life, karma, whatever. This approach has never let me down, and it has made all the difference in my life."

STEVE JOBS

"LIFE IS INHERENTLY RISKY.
THERE IS ONLY ONE BIG RISK
YOU SHOULD AVOID AT ALL
COSTS, AND THAT IS THE
RISK OF DOING NOTHING."

DENIS WAITLEY

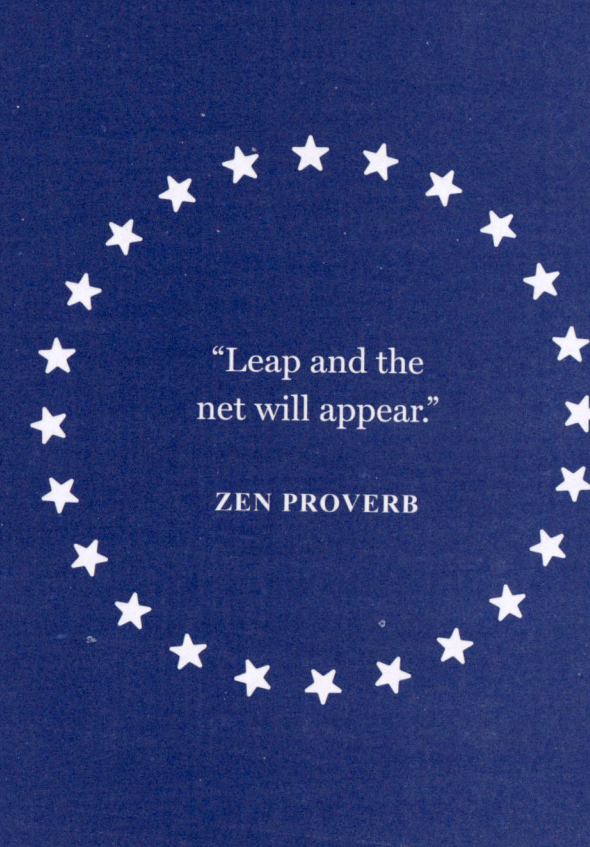

"Leap and the
net will appear."

ZEN PROVERB

"YOUR TIME IS LIMITED,
SO DON'T WASTE IT LIVING
SOMEONE ELSE'S LIFE."

Steve Jobs

"Every man dies, but not
every man really lives."

WILLIAM WALLACE

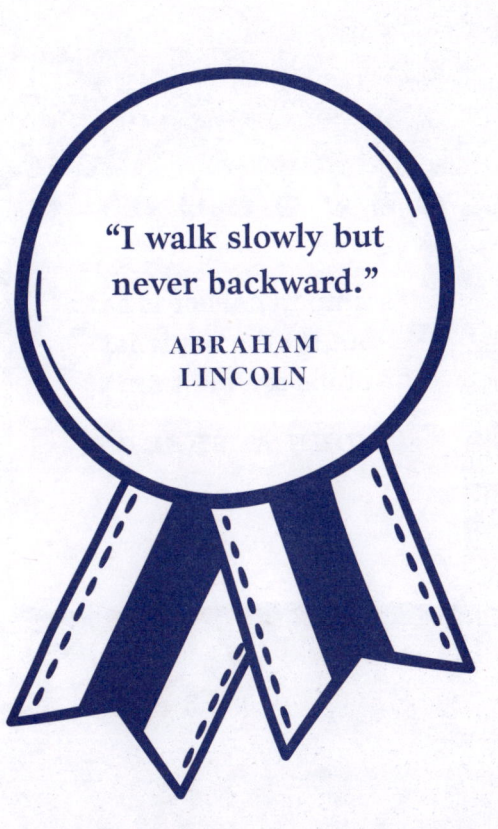

"I walk slowly but never backward."

ABRAHAM LINCOLN

"A ship in harbor is safe,
but that is not what
ships are built for."

JOHN A. SHEDD

"Don't worry about failures, worry about the chances you miss when you don't even try."

JACK CANFIELD

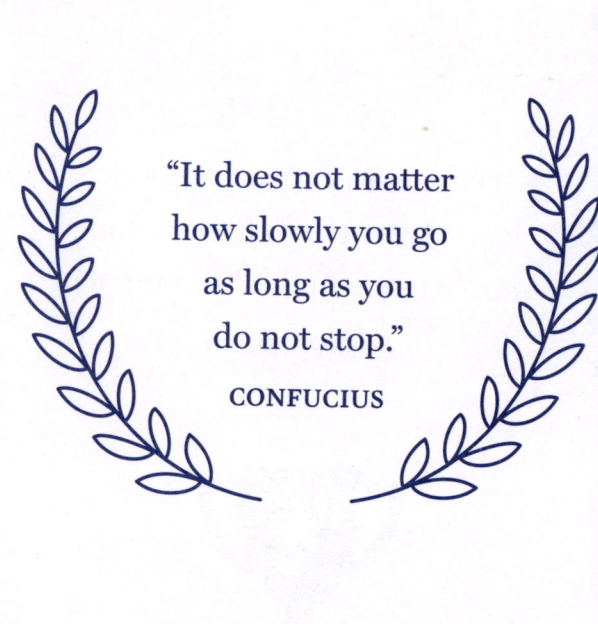

"It does not matter
how slowly you go
as long as you
do not stop."

CONFUCIUS

"THINK BIG AND DON'T
LISTEN TO PEOPLE WHO TELL
YOU IT CAN'T BE DONE.
LIFE IS TOO SHORT
TO THINK SMALL."

TIM FERRISS

"YOU NEVER KNOW WHAT
YOU CAN DO, UNTIL YOU TRY."

Anonymous

"Do one thing every day
that scares you."

ELEANOR
ROOSEVELT

"If you are not willing to risk
the unusual, you will have
to settle for the ordinary."

JIM ROHN

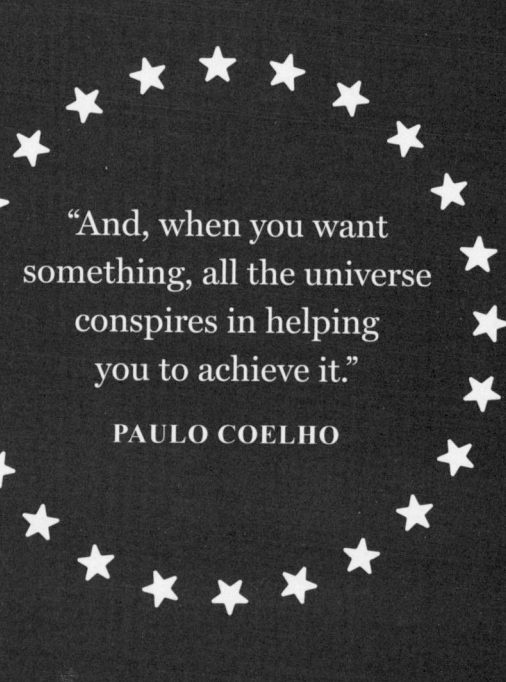

"And, when you want
something, all the universe
conspires in helping
you to achieve it."

PAULO COELHO

"It's hard to beat a person
who never gives up."

BABE RUTH

"Goal setting is the secret to a compelling future."

TONY ROBBINS

"Without hustle, talent will only carry you so far."

GARY VAYNERCHUK

"Success is the sum of small efforts, repeated day in and day out."

ROBERT COLLIER

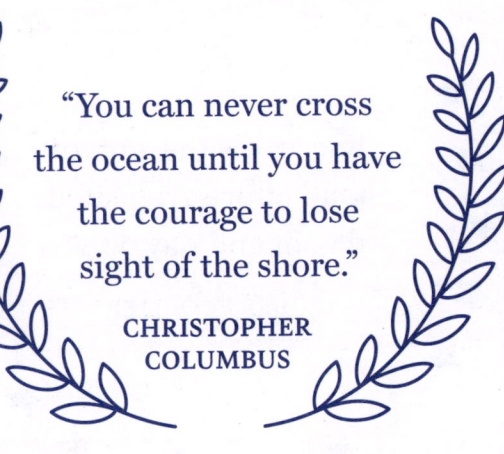

"You can never cross
the ocean until you have
the courage to lose
sight of the shore."

CHRISTOPHER
COLUMBUS

"IF MY MIND CAN CONCEIVE IT,
AND MY HEART CAN BELIEVE IT,
THEN I CAN ACHIEVE IT."

Muhammad Ali

"KEEP YOUR FACE ALWAYS
TOWARD THE SUNSHINE—AND
SHADOWS WILL FALL BEHIND YOU."

WALT WHITMAN

"The most important thing in life is to stop saying, 'I wish' and start saying, 'I will'. Consider nothing impossible, then treat possibilities as probabilities."

CHARLES DICKENS

"The journey of a thousand miles begins with one step."

LAO TZU

"Life is like riding a bicycle.
To keep your balance,
you must keep moving."

ALBERT EINSTEIN

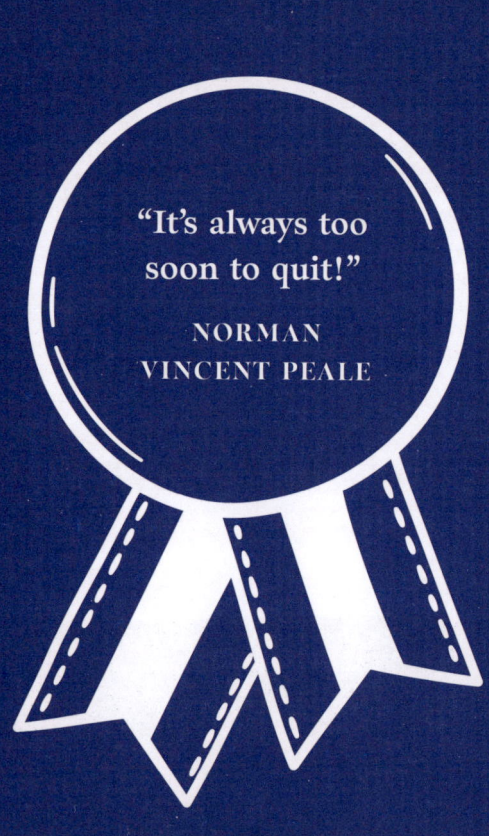

"It's always too soon to quit!"

NORMAN
VINCENT PEALE

"Strength does not come from winning. Your struggles develop your strengths. When you go through hardships and decide not to surrender, that is strength."

ARNOLD SCHWARZENEGGER

"IT IS NOT IN THE STARS
TO HOLD OUR DESTINY
BUT IN OURSELVES."

**WILLIAM
SHAKESPEARE**

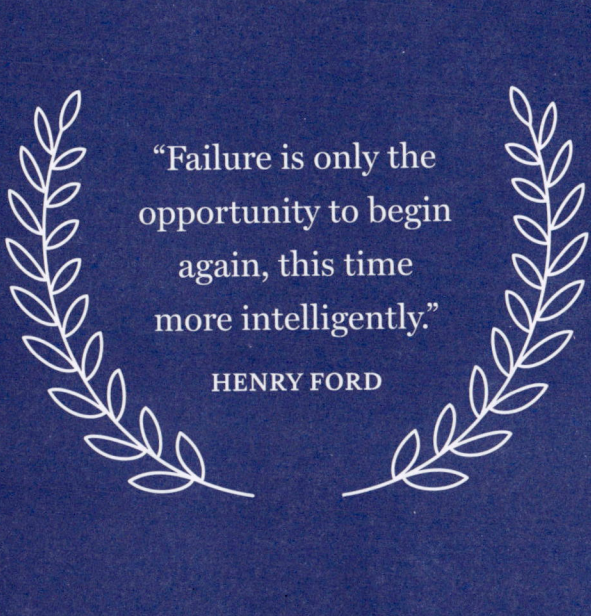

"Failure is only the
opportunity to begin
again, this time
more intelligently."

HENRY FORD

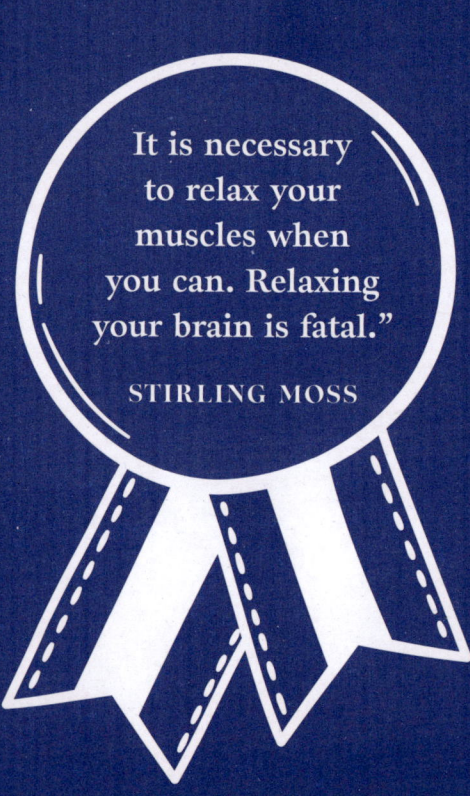

It is necessary to relax your muscles when you can. Relaxing your brain is fatal."

STIRLING MOSS

"No, you don't have to start
your play with a premise.
You can start with a character
or an incident, or even a simple
thought. This thought or incident
grows, and the story slowly
unfolds itself. You have time
to find your premise in the
mass of your material later.
The important thing is to find it."

LAJOS EGRI

"It is vain to say
human beings ought to be
satisfied with tranquility;
they must have action;
and they will make it
if they cannot find it."

CHARLOTTE BRONTE

"If you set goals and go after them with all the determination you can muster, your gifts will take you places that will amaze you."

LES BROWN

"ACTION MAY NOT ALWAYS BRING HAPPINESS; BUT THERE IS NO HAPPINESS WITHOUT ACTION."

Benjamin Disraeli

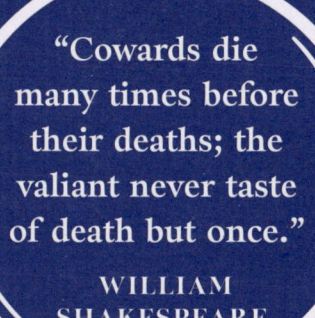

"Cowards die
many times before
their deaths; the
valiant never taste
of death but once."

WILLIAM
SHAKESPEARE

"First forget inspiration.
Habit is more dependable.
Habit will sustain you
whether you're inspired or not.
Habit will help you finish
and polish your stories.
Inspiration won't.
Habit is persistence in practice."

OCTAVIA E. BUTLER

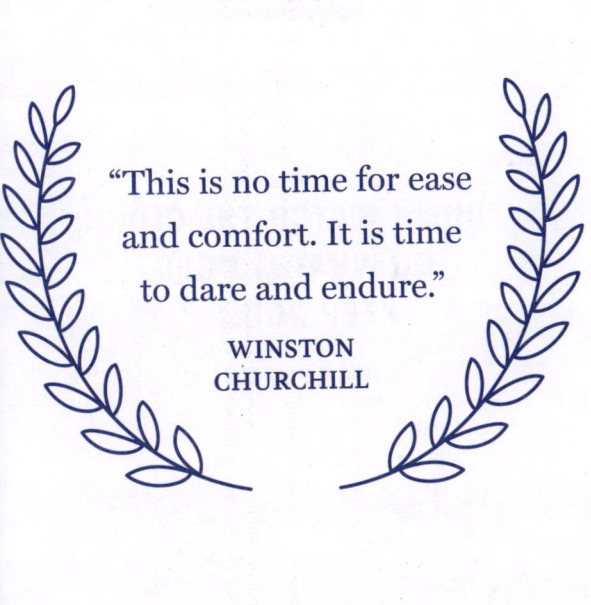

"This is no time for ease and comfort. It is time to dare and endure."

WINSTON CHURCHILL

"DON'T WATCH THE CLOCK;
DO WHAT IT DOES.
KEEP GOING."

SAM LEVENSON

"If you want something you've never had, you must be willing to do something you've never done."

THOMAS JEFFERSON

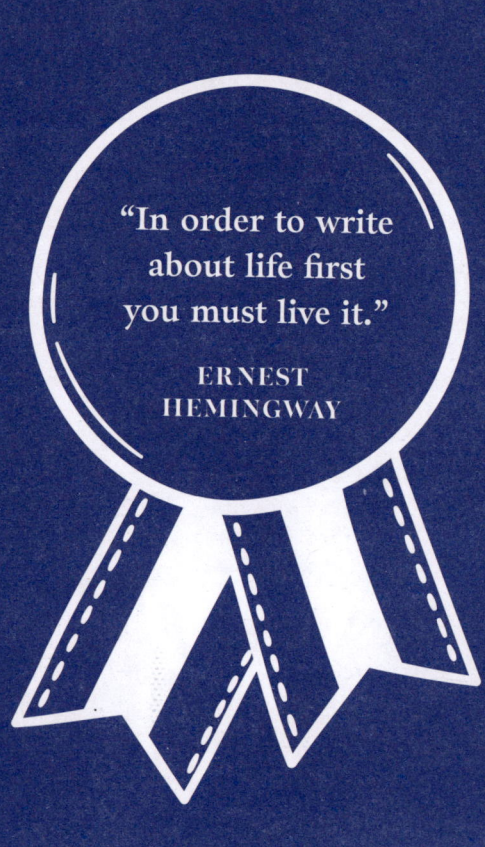

"In order to write
about life first
you must live it."

ERNEST
HEMINGWAY

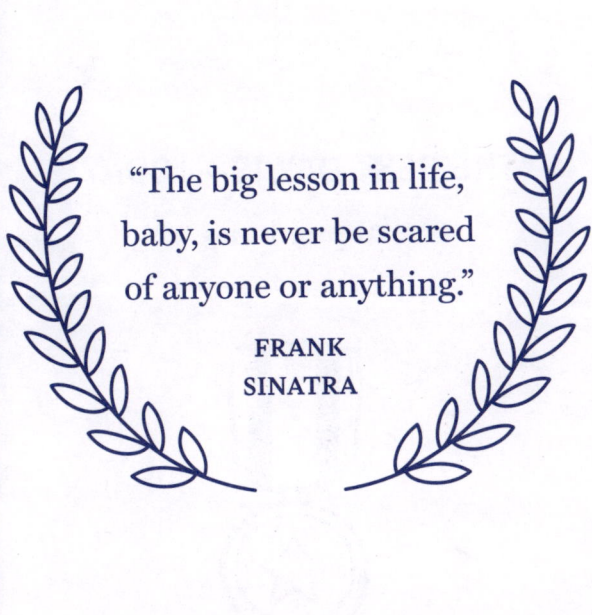

"The big lesson in life,
baby, is never be scared
of anyone or anything."

**FRANK
SINATRA**

"THE BEST DAY IS—TODAY!"

Anonymous

"Yesterday is ashes,
tomorrow wood.
Only today does the
fire burn brightly."

ESKIMO PROVERB

"DO THE BEST YOU CAN UNTIL
YOU KNOW BETTER. THEN WHEN
YOU KNOW BETTER, DO BETTER."

MAYA ANGELOU

"People who say it
cannot be done should
not interrupt those
who are doing it."

GEORGE
BERNARD SHAW

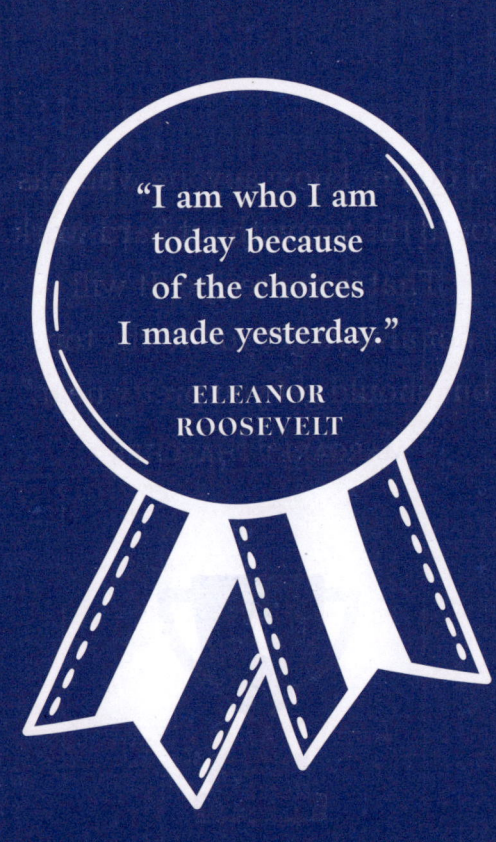

"I am who I am today because of the choices I made yesterday."

ELEANOR ROOSEVELT

"I do not know anyone who has got to the top without hard work. That is the recipe. It will not always get you to the top, but should get you pretty near."

MARGARET THATCHER

"Although you should
never mention your premise
in the dialogue of your play,
the audience must know
what the message is.
And whatever it is,
you must prove it."

LAJOS EGRI

"You can do it.
I can do it.
Let's do it."

SHERMAN ALEXIE

"I'M A GREAT BELIEVER
IN LUCK, AND I FIND THE
HARDER I WORK, THE
MORE I HAVE OF IT."

Thomas Jefferson

"He who is not courageous enough to take risks will accomplish nothing in life."

MUHAMMAD ALI

"All our dreams can come true, if we have the courage to pursue them."

WALT DISNEY

"The greater the
difficulty, the
more the glory in
surmounting it."

EPICURUS

"The fact is, that to do anything in the world worth doing, we must not stand back shivering and thinking of the cold and danger, but jump in and scramble through as well as we can."

ROBERT CUSHING

"Our greatest weakness lies in giving up. The most certain way to succeed is always to try just one more time."

THOMAS A. EDISON

"MOST OF THE IMPORTANT
THINGS IN THE WORLD HAVE
BEEN ACCOMPLISHED BY
PEOPLE WHO HAVE KEPT ON
TRYING WHEN THERE SEEMED
TO BE NO HOPE AT ALL."

DALE CARNEGIE

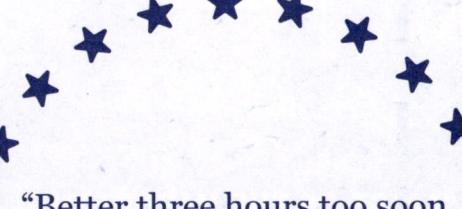

"Better three hours too soon
than a minute too late."

WILLIAM SHAKESPEARE

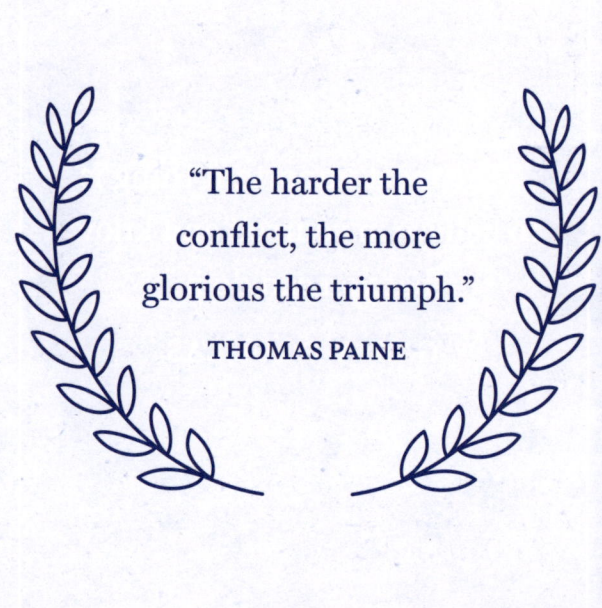

"The harder the conflict, the more glorious the triumph."

THOMAS PAINE

"The most important thing is
to believe in yourself and know
that you can do it."

GABBY DOUGLAS

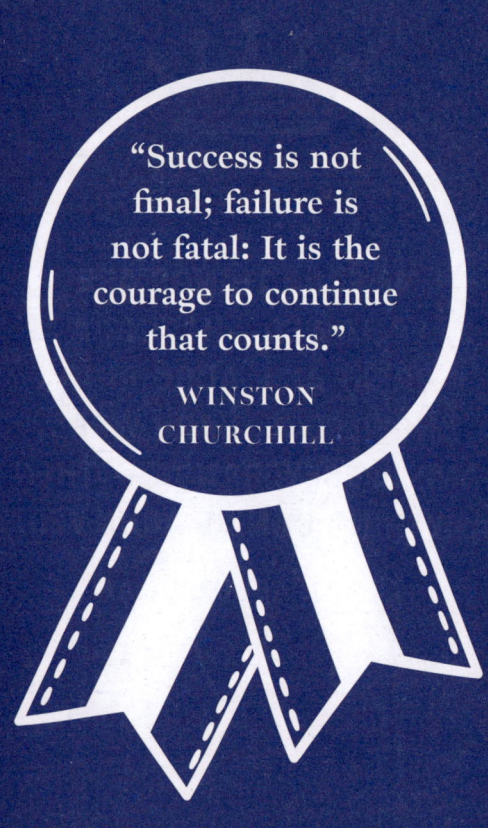

"Success is not final; failure is not fatal: It is the courage to continue that counts."

WINSTON CHURCHILL

"IF FOUR THINGS ARE FOLLOWED—HAVING A GREAT AIM, ACQUIRING KNOWLEDGE, HARD WORK, AND PERSEVERANCE — THEN ANYTHING CAN BE ACHIEVED."

A. P. J. ABDUL KALAM

"If a man is called to be a street
sweeper, he should sweep streets
even as Michelangelo painted,
or Beethoven played music,
or Shakespeare wrote poetry.
He should sweep streets so well
that all the hosts of heaven and
earth will pause to say, 'Here
lived a great street sweeper
who did his job well.'"

MARTIN LUTHER KING JR.

"Don't be too timid and squeamish about your actions. All life is an experiment. The more experiments you make the better."

RALPH WALDO EMERSON

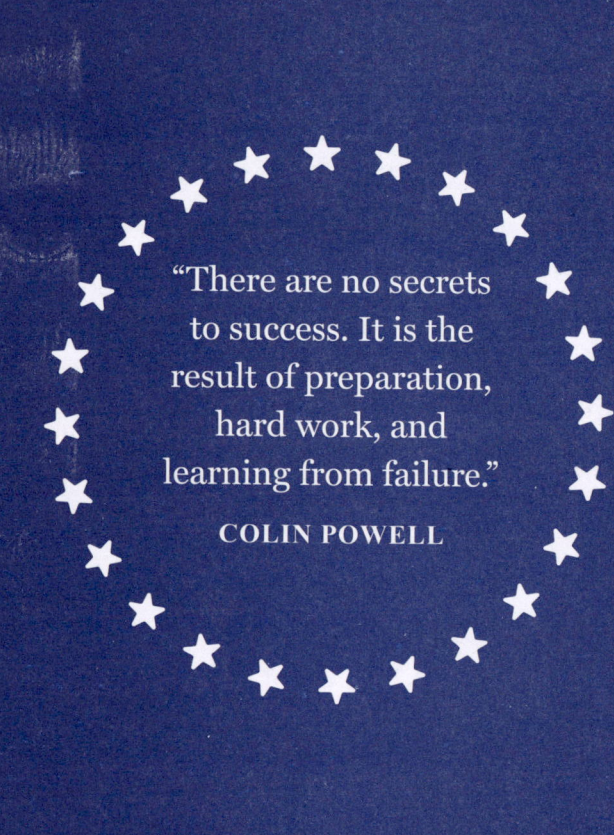

"There are no secrets
to success. It is the
result of preparation,
hard work, and
learning from failure."

COLIN POWELL

"Success is to be measured not so much by the position that one has reached in life as by the obstacles which he has overcome while trying to succeed."

BOOKER T. WASHINGTON

"THERE ARE ONLY TWO MISTAKES ONE CAN MAKE ALONG THE ROAD TO TRUTH; NOT GOING ALL THE WAY, AND NOT STARTING."

Buddha

"He who would learn to
fly one day must first learn
to stand and walk and run
and climb and dance;
one cannot fly into flying."

FRIEDRICH NIETZSCHE

"PERSEVERANCE IS NOT
A LONG RACE;
IT IS MANY SHORT RACES
ONE AFTER THE OTHER."

WALTER ELLIOT

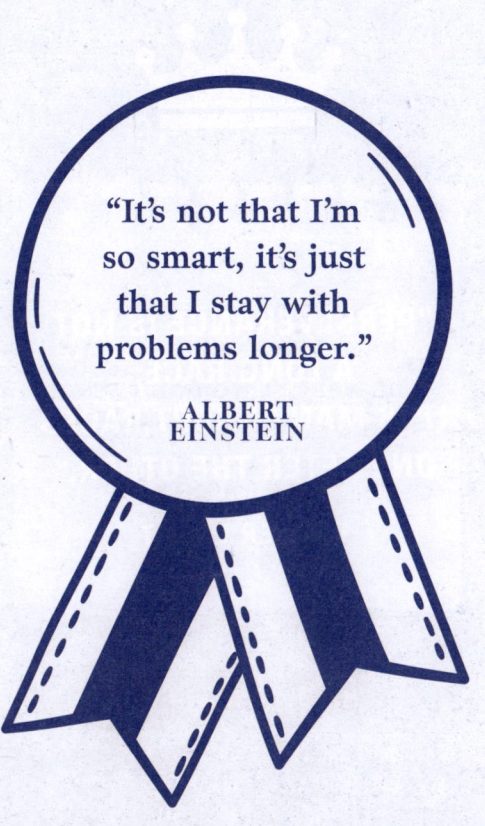

"It's not that I'm so smart, it's just that I stay with problems longer."

ALBERT EINSTEIN

"If people knew how hard I worked to get my mastery, it wouldn't seem so wonderful after all."

MICHELANGELO

AFFIRMATIONS TO BOOST YOUR SELF ESTEEM

★ I am confident, capable, and strong.

★ I will be kind to myself.

★ I grow and learn from each challenge that comes my way.

★ I have what it takes to achieve my goals and fulfill my dreams.

★ I am the only one who gets to determine my self-worth.

★ No matter what negative thoughts tell me, I will cultivate a positive and optimistic mindset.

★ Success is a subjective notion and I define my success on my terms.

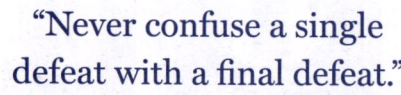

"Never confuse a single
defeat with a final defeat."

F. SCOTT FITZGERALD

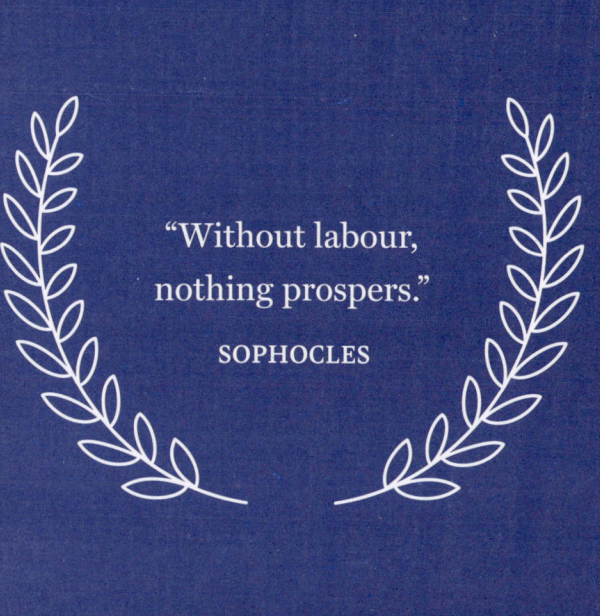

"Without labour,
nothing prospers."

SOPHOCLES

"The only difference between success and failure is the ability to take action."

ALEXANDER GRAHAM BELL

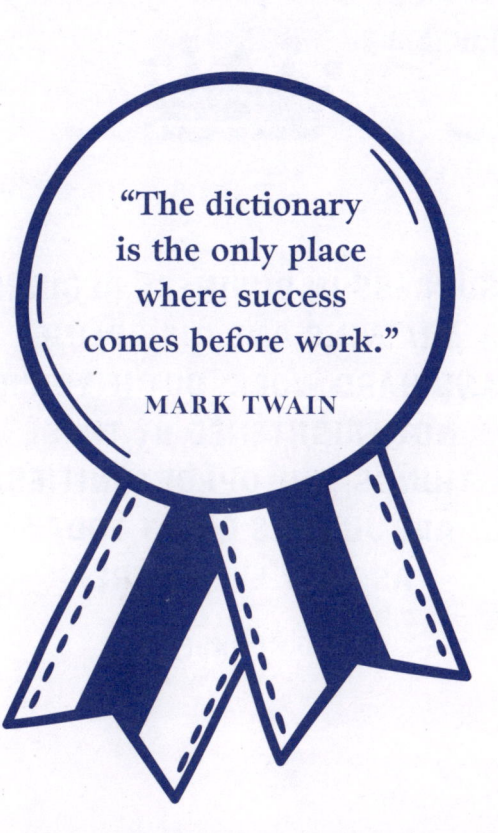

"The dictionary is the only place where success comes before work."

MARK TWAIN

"SUCCESS IN BUSINESS REQUIRES
TRAINING AND DISCIPLINE,
AND HARD WORK. BUT IF YOU'RE
NOT FRIGHTENED BY THESE
THINGS, THE OPPORTUNITIES
ARE JUST AS GREAT TODAY
AS THEY EVER WERE."

DAVID ROCKEFELLER

"CHARACTER CANNOT
BE DEVELOPED IN EASE
AND QUIET. ONLY THROUGH
EXPERIENCE OF TRIAL AND
SUFFERING CAN THE SOUL
BE STRENGTHENED, VISION
CLEARED, AMBITION INSPIRED
AND SUCCESS ACHIEVED."

HELEN KELLER

"It is better to conquer
yourself than to win
a thousand battles.
Then the victory is yours.
It cannot be taken from
you, not by angels or by
demons, heaven or hell."

BUDDHA

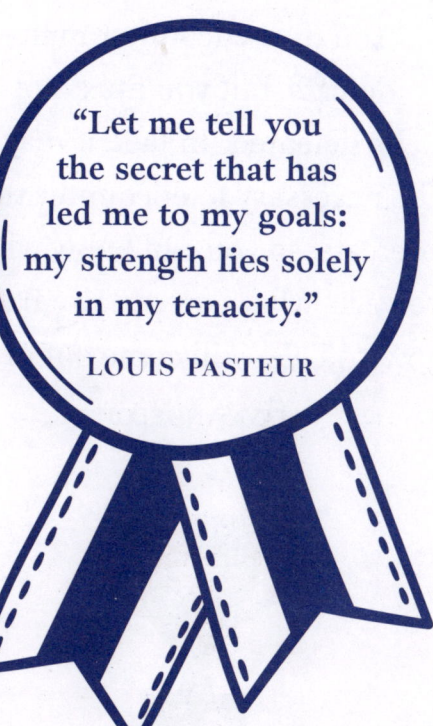

"Let me tell you the secret that has led me to my goals: my strength lies solely in my tenacity."

LOUIS PASTEUR

"You may encounter many defeats, but you must not be defeated. In fact, it may be necessary to encounter the defeats, so you can know who you are, what you can rise from, how you can still come out of it."

MAYA ANGELOU

"Always do your best.
What you plant now,
you will harvest later."

OG MANDINO

"You can't turn back
the clock. But you
can wind it up again."

BONNIE PRUDDEN

"A little more persistence, a little more effort and what seemed hopeless failure may turn to glorious success."

ELBERT HUBBARD

"The fight is won or lost far away from witnesses—behind the lines, in the gym, and out there on the road, long before I dance under those lights."

MUHAMMAD ALI

"ETERNITY IS AN ENDLESS
CHAIN OF NOWS."

ANONYMOUS

"It always seems
impossible until it is done."

NELSON MANDELA

"A BEND IN THE ROAD
IS NOT THE END OF THE
ROAD . . . UNLESS YOU FAIL
TO MAKE THE TURN."

Helen Keller

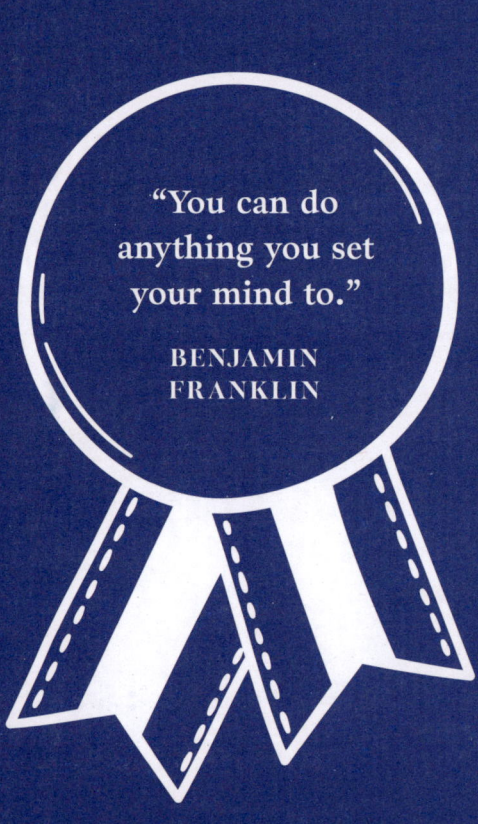

"You can do anything you set your mind to."

BENJAMIN
FRANKLIN

"The only guarantee for failure is to stop trying."

JOHN C. MAXWELL

"MANY OF LIFE'S FAILURES ARE PEOPLE WHO DID NOT REALISE HOW CLOSE THEY WERE TO SUCCESS WHEN THEY GAVE UP."

THOMAS A. EDISON

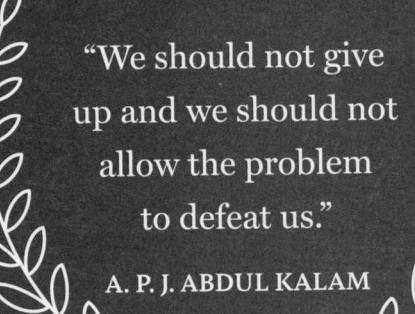

"We should not give
up and we should not
allow the problem
to defeat us."

A. P. J. ABDUL KALAM

"Success is no accident. It is hard work, perseverance, learning, studying, sacrifice and most of all, love of what you are doing or learning to do."

PELE

"Fall seven times and stand up eight."

JAPANESE PROVERB

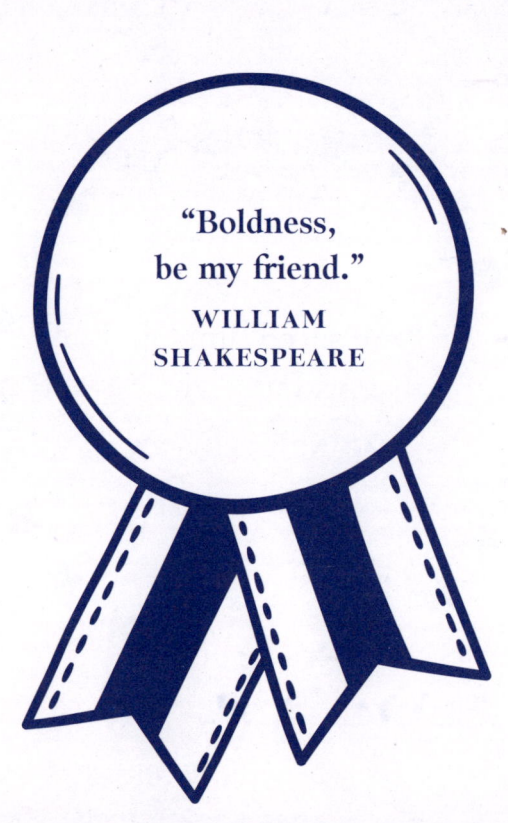

"Boldness,
be my friend."

WILLIAM
SHAKESPEARE

"Develop success from failures. Discouragement and failure are two of the surest stepping stones to success."

DALE CARNEGIE

"You've done it before
and you can do it now.
See the positive possibilities.
Redirect the substantial energy
of your frustration and turn
it into positive, effective,
unstoppable determination."

RALPH MARSTON

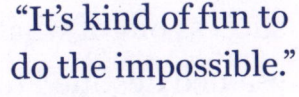

"It's kind of fun to
do the impossible."

WALT DISNEY

"Through perseverance
many people win
success out of what
seemed destined to
be certain failure."

**BENJAMIN
DISRAELI**

"FAILURE IS OFTEN THAT
EARLY MORNING HOUR
OF DARKNESS WHICH
PRECEDES THE DAWNING
OF THE DAY OF SUCCESS."

Leigh Mitchell Hodges

"The only impossible
journey is the one
you never begin."

TONY ROBBINS

"Our future accomplishments are determined entirely by how every second in our life is put to use. The future is the cumulation of many nows."

ANONYMOUS

"MOTIVATION COMES
FROM WORKING ON THINGS
WE CARE ABOUT."

SHERYL SANDBERG

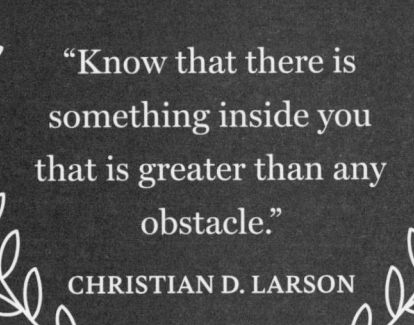

"Know that there is something inside you that is greater than any obstacle."

CHRISTIAN D. LARSON

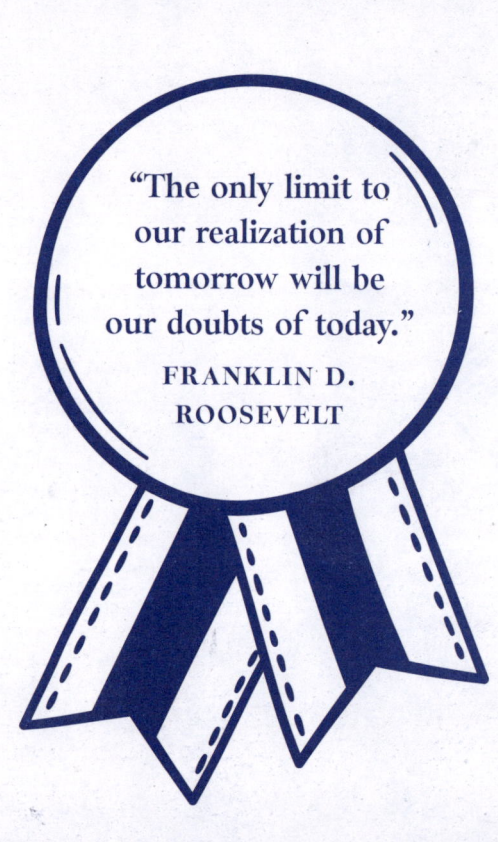

"The only limit to our realization of tomorrow will be our doubts of today."

FRANKLIN D. ROOSEVELT